When Monday Comes

By: Jacqueline Loh

Grace that Reigns Society

When Monday Comes

ISBN 978-1-9995427-0-2

This Personal Catholic *Vade Mecum*
(A take me with you spiritual book) belongs to:

_____

With God… All things are Possible.

Matt 19:26

I would urge those who hear of you to take that leap of Faith into the Holy Spirit who breathes afresh through you. Priests and People will benefit from the Sense of Wonder the two of you bring to Faith, to Church, and to life.

The late, Most Reverend Eugene J. Gerber

Bishop Emeritus of Wichita, Kansas

I received numerous expressions of appreciation for the presentations that Bishop Gilmore and Jacqueline Loh gave during our Lenten Retreat. I remain grateful that you will continue to in this ministry. I believe that the model of a bishop and lay-woman working collaboratively for the enrichment of parish life provides an example that can challenge how ministry in parishes should be exercised.

Most Reverend Thomas J. Olmsted
Bishop of Phoenix, Arizona

I was overwhelmed by the positive feedback I received from many of my parishioners. I understand that practically everyone in attendance took the opportunity to spend time with Jacqueline in prayer but also spent time with Bishop Gilmore in Confession.

Fr. Sergio Munoz Fita
St. Anne Roman Catholic Parish
Gilbert, Arizona

The people who attend the Mission said that they had learned a lot to enhance their spiritual lives. Please keep up your good work of making Christ's grace alive in our hearts.

Fr. Thomas Smith
St Francis de Sales Parish
Burnaby, British Columbia

I loved having 2 perspectives on each topic. I loved that the information presented was on our "level". The way the nights were offered, we were able to talk about it at home. The format is very relaxing and peaceful. There was so many good insights to it. The presenters were very good together.

Elaina Flann
Sacred Heart Parish
Prescott, Arizona

I enjoyed it very much and all the basic reminders of the meaning of Advent. Very thoughtful and provoking retreat given by the presenters. I liked the gentleness of the presenters but also their empathetic way of making their points. We were blessed to have Bishop Gilmore and Jacqueline Loh at our Parish.

John and Genesta King
St Mary's Catholic Church
Ponca City, Oklahoma

" It was awesome. I felt many 'aaaah' moments. The Spirit was moving me. Especially I enjoyed adoration/exposition of the Eucharist and the healing session. It was powerful and peaceful. The combination of Bishop Gilmore and Jacqueline was so great."

Carey Boyzuch
Wichita Spiritual Life Centre
Wichita, Kansas

When Monday Comes

By: Jacqueline Loh
Grace that Reigns Society

Hello friend. So when was the last time you had an awe-inspiring moment that made you say "WOW!" and le t you in awe and reverence? The Grand Canyon, or the Great Wall of China can do that. But a religious experience can also do that too!

A religious experience did that for me. I have always belonged to the Catholic faith, but I will never forget one powerful experience of the presence of God that left me speechless. I felt like a child again, seeing myself as with simplicity and feeling His loving presence with a deep emotion of awe.

Although I experienced other moments of closeness with God; they never compared to those first experiences.

Through the years, as " life " got in the way, I wanted to re-capture that original sense of awe, reverence and wonder that came with the realization that God loved me, and that He was *alive* in my life. I felt sparkly, unique and *loved*. That moment changed me. It made me look into myself and realize that I was not the centre of the universe and that God had plans for me. That experience gave me a desire to reach out to help others to re-capture, and re-ignite their first encounter, with a new freshness and boldness for themselves, and their faith, that would spur them on towards their calling.

Soon after, starting in 2008, I felt the Lord calling me to grow a ministry based entirely on *"Renewing Wonder." I prayed a lot about it and wrote my first inspired words at a monastery in Northern Ireland.* Bishop Gilmore joined Grace that Reigns in September of 2012.

We, Bishop Ronal Gilmore and I at *Grace that Reigns* want to help you to renew your own wonder for God's love for you and help you begin your **new adventure**.

This book is the fruit of our labour, in collaboration with God's grace: over 15 years of individual ministry for me, and almost 50 years for Bishop Gilmore, with both priests and people. It also bears witness to the past 7 years of our collaboration together at *Grace that Reigns*.

We want to help you recognize: that God loves you and He is there present in you; that he works in your lives in many ways; and that there are many barriers, or stumbling blocks, which will get in the way of his work within you. We want to help you see again the many mysteries that surrounded you at your making, to help you identify them, and to bring God's healing and peace to you and to those you love.

We want *When Monday Comes* to open your understanding of just how unique you are. We want it to allow you to see yourself as God sees you, with a deep unconditional love, and as a *Pearl of Great Price*. We want it to fill your love of the Lord with a new kind of reverence.

Are you ready to allow the Lord in, to move forward on your spiritual journey, with a new freshness, and boldness, and rhythm to your step? I am not alone on an island.

Many people have come and gone, and have helped me. I want to thank Dr. Gerry Doran personally: he has supported me with his time, patience, incredible giftedness, and friendship through the years, he has helped me believe in myself. Without him, this ministry would not exist. I also remember fondly, and give thanks to the late Fr. Kevin Scallon CM, founder of the *Intercession for Priests* for inviting me to Ireland and encouraging, and then accompanying me on my spiritual journey. Then came Archbishop Michael Miller from the Archdiocese of Vancouver, Canada - and Bishop John Brungardt from the Diocese of Dodge City, Kansas for opening up their doors to *Grace that Reigns*.

I must thank too, my sister, Juliana, my parents, and many wonderful and prayerful good friends from the very beginning of this ministry.

Also, Amy Leung, our wonderful graphic artist, with her fine feel for the look of this book and Kathy Shantz, our first editorial eye.

I *especially* want to thank our sponsors; without them, and their financial gifts, *our ministry could not survive*

Finally, last but not least... Bishop Ronald Gilmore: my spiritual partner. He too helped me to believe in myself, and to trust the God who was speaking to me. His thoughts, especially on Spiritual Direction and Consolation and Desolation have also been added to this book.

You would not have what you now hold, without them.

Jacqueline Loh B.A B.L.Arch
Grace that Reigns Society
Founder

When you lose your sense of that first love of God, or of his continuing grace and presence in your life, or of your original sense of simplicity, you are on the way to losing your sense of wonder. When that happens, it is easy to miss the clues to the mysteries God wants in your life.

The kingdom of heaven is like a merchant seeking beautiful pearls, who, when he had found one pearl of great price, went and sold all that he had and bought it.

Matt 13:45-46

Are you ready to begin your Journey with us?

Many of us have allowed routine and habit to take over our lives.

When we wake up, go to school, go to work, attend meetings, tackle our lists, it is easy to forget about the ways through which God is present throughout the day. Over time we can become numb to his love, his presence, and the wonder of his gifts. Life can become mundane as we can fall " out of Love " with our Creator and Redeemer. When this happens, it can be harder to remain alive to your new day, and to the new things God will give you in it.

That is why Jesus loved little children through all his life. Have you ever watched a child at the beach when she finds a shiny shell? Have you ever watched when he stops and marvels at the slightest of things, and examines them with great interest?

Children give free reign to their quiet innocence. They take time to inhale all the shape, color, meaning, and beauty of Creation. You can see them with all five senses alert and tingling: seeing, hearing, tasting, touching and smelling. They live in the moment and they notice even the littlest things in it. Children are connected to the purer emotions of their hearts, and that leaves them open to all the gifts of the Spirit of God.

The more we mature, the more we are inclined to use our heads to experience the world, rather than our hearts. **Simplicity** is the key to being open to wonder and its movement within us. **Simplicity uncomplicates our spiritual journey, and as we move towards heaven, renewing wonder becomes ever so important.**

Photo Courtesy of Amy Obregon

Our Goal is dedicated to "Renewing Wonder."

Above all else, we want you to go beyond the narrow comfort of your everyday routine, and to recover a Sense of Wonder in your lives: Wonder at God, at your Faith, at your life of Prayer, at what you see in front of you, and at the people around you, and especially at yourself, and your own personal and mysterious adventure with Christ.

Q: What is my take away from this retreat?

1. You will recall the first time you knew that Jesus loved you, and that you were not alone. You will also recall the first time you fell in love with Jesus

2. You will find solutions to your real life problems and understand the unfolding of God's grace during this directed retreat.

3. You will be given opportunities to dig deeper by asking

questions, by facing your own insecurities, and by finding encouragement from those around you in these retreat hours.

4. You will identify the barriers that hold you back from loving Jesus to the full.

5. You will learn to move away from old negative patterns, and move towards developing new positive patterns that will solidify your view of yourself and your *trust* in Jesus Christ.

6. You will become alert to what Grace is, and you will receive God's Grace and Healing.

7. You will meet various Saints who will share with you how they coped with the very obstacles you now face.

8. You will receive healing prayer, and there will be times for Confession.

9. You will learn how to recognize your own gifts and talents. In re-learning how to love Jesus more fully, you will be guided by the Holy Spirit to use your talents to the fullest experience of joy.

Q: Why is Renewing Wonder so important?

Wonder tends to get lost when we are too caught up in the things of this world. When that happens, we begin to miss things. We miss the presence of Christ's love, and the prayer his love inspires. We miss the beauty of our environment, and the beauty of one another. And we miss the strange new world of the Liturgy, the sounds and the gestures of the Eucharist and the Sacraments.

What the gift of wonder does is, it lifts us up beyond what we are comfortable with and helps us to realize what or who is in front of us. Ultimately, it lets us see beyond ourselves, and how we might bring our talents, gifts, and charisms into our communities.

Q: What is the Church's view on Wonder?

Wonder has another name in the sevenfold gifts of the Holy Spirit: there it is called Fear. But it is not the negative fears that we know so well. It is rather the feeling of being in the presence of something bigger than we are: it is a mix of respect, and reverence, and awe. It is, well, **Wonder**.

When any Bishop prepares to anoint those to be confirmed with the Sacred Chrism, he holds out his hands and prays,

All powerful God, Father of our Lord Jesus Christ, by water and the Holy Spirit you freed your sons and daughters from sin and gave them new life. Send your Holy Spirit upon them to be their helper and guide. Give them the spirit of wisdom and understanding, the spirit of right judgement and courage, the spirit of knowledge and reverence. Fill them with the spirit of wonder and awe in your presence. We ask this through Christ our Lord. Amen

Q: Why was this workbook named "When Monday Comes?"

Following the *Miracle Worker*, the movie about Helen Keller's coming to herself through the work of her skilled teacher, there was a second movie about her slow, hard, emergence into adulthood. It was called *Monday after the Miracle*, a lovely phrase suggestive of the hard everydayness of life. After the magic moment when she was finally able to overcome her blindness and deafness, and to communicate with the world, we see the day to day struggles of the rest of her life.

When Monday Comes is our take on the long, and sometimes difficult, struggles after that initial magic of your conversion experience, when life gets in the way, and God seems not so close anymore. This book will help you understand the ups and the downs of that journey, will help you not to be afraid of them, and will help you know what to do about them. As such, it is filled with hope, and with healing.

Q: What's Inside?

We invite you to re-discover three topics: *Love, Wonder, and Grace.* You will then be introduced to the topic of *Spiritual Direction*, what it is, and how we can accompany you during your time with us.

Next, we explore the topic of prayer and the patterns of prayer, its up-times, and its down-times, what St. Ignatius called *consolation* and *desolation.*

You will then be introduced to *Sin*, and the *Obstacles* and *Barriers* that challenge your growing relationship with Christ. We will discuss four major obstacles: fear, control, unworthiness, and finally resentment/ forgiveness. As you come to terms with these four obstacles, you will be provided with Scripture passages, and ideas, to help reveal the mystery surrounding you unfold.

Once you feel comfortable with the format, we offer you a list of other obstacles for you to check off and evaluate on your own or in a group. With it, we highly recommend a book called, *"Saintly Solutions to Life's Common Problems."*

The workbook concludes with a discussion on *Healing*, a final prayer, a section on *journeying towards consolation*, followed by, *discovering your own personal talents and gifts*. The retreat book concludes with, *"Where do I go from here?"*

Q: How can this workbook help me?

We want to accompany you on this journey by sharing all we have
learned in the last seven years of offering retreats, healing prayers,
and spiritual direction. This book takes what we heard from you, and
others like you, takes what we have seen the Lord do in you to make
his mysterious presence known through his healing and grace. It
helps you cope with all your Mondays, and thus to find your sense of
wonder again. Use this book to record your own spiritual journey.

*God builds his house. True, he asks us to cooperate with him, but we do not
do the essential building. Where people let themselves be claimed by God,
where they have time for him, where they make space for him, there they
are on the way to building the House of God-with-us.* (Bishop Gilmore)

Q: How Do I Use this retreat book?

As you notice, this book is divided into a number of sections.

Each section of the workbook is divided into various topics. There is a
description for each topic; followed by an example of what it looks
like. The next section is titled, questions to ask yourself. Finally,
a scripture or quote is included, along with a healing prayer and
suggested readings.

After the retreat, we would also recommend that you take it home
and discuss one section at a time with your friends, or several sections
if time permits. The main idea is for you to gain as much as you can,
by reflecting on each section yourself, or with others.

In speaking of the Spiritual Director, the Catechism of the Catholic Church says that the "Holy Spirit gives [some of the faithful] the gifts of wisdom, faith, and discernment for the sake of the common good which is prayer." In other words, mature Christians with these gifts are able to help others grow closer to God through prayer. [CCC 2690]

Basic guidelines when working with spiritual directors

We are made to know, love, and serve God in this life, and to be happy with him in the next. If we miss that, we miss everything, the whole point of why we were made. And we run the risk of missing the communion to which he calls us.

The *Director* who most helps us stay on point is the Spirit of God, poured into us at our own Baptism. He is there at the beginning, at the middle, and at the end of our journey. There are many reasons why we often miss his quiet guidance, some are our fault, and some are not.

The Church has come to think that human spiritual directors are also useful for each person's journey. It is very easy to delude our-selves in spiritual matters. Another set of eyes, another voice, another mind, this is one of the best helps against such delusion. Familiar with God, and the things of God, and the ways of God, he or she can be a boon companion.

Familiar with the women and men of the world, and the things of the world, and the ways of the world, she or he can be a vigilant scout to warn us of dangers here and dangers there. They can hold up a mirror, objective and unblinking, so that you can see how you are relating to God, and how you do too often lose your way in illusion.

We want to make plain to you that when the human director senses the presence of the Divine Director, she has the good sense to fall silent, he has the good sense to get out of the way. They don't want to mar the delicate masterpiece the Lord is Himself, creating.

We want to enhance your prayer life, which nourishes and sustains the life of the entire Church. We want to help you hear and obey God's call, and to carry out your particular vocation. We want you help you to fall in love again, and to follow where that Love leads you.

Seeking Direction

1. People seeking direction will share their encounters with the divine, and will show how they are cultivating a life attuned to spiritual things.

2. While experiencing this workshop, you will be shown elements of what we ourselves offer when we give Spiritual Direction to individuals.

3. If you have chosen to experience this workshop with others in your parish, or in the comfort of your own home, and you do not have a spiritual director, this guide will help you review your own journey of prayer, and help to detect where the Lord is taking you. Through reflection, conversation, and prayer, you will be able to find clarity about your life's journey. Remember it is your journey, and your Director in the end is the Spirit of God.

4. Take time to absorb and to write whatever comes to mind about your personal experiences, and about where the road seems to be taking you. This will help you detect patterns in your prayer and life.

In case you don't have a spiritual director right now, don't worry about it. Go through the topics, discuss them with your friends, complete the questions, read our resources and the information we provide in our website, and reflect and pray on your own.

After all this, you will probably want to consult a priest, sister or lay person to answer your questions, or to help you to go forward in your spiritual journey. Illusion is always a real and present danger.

But remember..."God is in charge of your life, and the Holy Spirit will lead you."

The first, and greatest, commandment is to **Love God with all your heart and all your soul.** The second is to **Love your neighbor as you love yourself.** These were the greatest in the Old Testament, these were confirmed as the greatest in the New Testament by Jesus himself.

One thing we frequently ask at our retreats is, "*When was the last time you fell in love with God and realized that he was truly alive?*" We ask that because most of us realize that God loves us, but we are not always receptive to that love, and active in it. Our need to give thanks and to praise should always be bubbling up in us. That's the way we return his love. God loved us first, the New Testament tells us, and we should "praise God forever and ever" (Daniel 20:30).

I will never forget the moment when I recognized that not only did God love me, but, most importantly, **I LOVED him!** It happened at the Old Spaghetti Factory in Vancouver when my sister and I had gone out to celebrate our recent conversion experience. She and I were waiting to be served, and I remember consciously inviting Jesus to dine with us because I knew he was in my life and that I loved him so very much. So we set out an empty chair and placed it beside us and asked him to sit with us. It was a gesture of complete surrender and gratitude. Now when I look back, it was an act of child-like simplicity. We laughed and were so filled with joy that night. Somehow through the years, my original sense of wonder began to ebb and to flow, to start and to stop, and then to grow again. It has never been static. When life gets overwhelming, I remember that initial experience, and yearn for it yet again.

Love is a theme that you see literally everywhere. It fills our movies, our songs, and our novels. No television show is without it, no poem, no play: it even has its own Holiday on St. Valentine's day, though it is now politically correct to leave the Saint-part out of it.

The word "love" is used so loosely that it is almost too ubiquitous. We hear most people say *I love you* to the people they love. But what do they usually mean? *I love you, because you make me happy. I love you because you complete me. I love you because you satisfy me.*

That can't be true love, because it is all about what another person can do for me. True love is about the other person.

What is Love?

True love is a sacrificial love: it puts the other person first, not ourselves. True love is what God did for us when he offered us his Son as his ultimate sacrifice. **He loved until it hurt, he took a quick breath, and then he went on to love us to the end.**

True love is a giving of self, not just of our material goods. It is shown in the giving of our time, and energy, and effort, and freedom, without asking or expecting anything back in return. True love is a sacrificial giving from our hearts. The truest form of authentic love was shown in the sacrifice of Jesus on the cross for our sins and for our salvation. This ultimate sacrifice is worth meditating on so that we can grasp its purest form.

What does it look like?

When we think of an emotionally healthy mother or father with their children, we can see how much they pour themselves out in order to love and protect their children. It is not about them: it is never about them. It is about the others, the helpless children.

Through their actions, nearly always sacrificial, parents give constantly and unconditionally to their children from the time they are babies until they are mature young adults. That love is wholly sacrificial. It is deep, protective, and beautiful. That is the way God loves us.

Questions to Ask Yourself:

1. When was the first time I recognized in your heart, that I loved God?

2. In what ways did I draw closer to him?

3. What does true love look like to me? Is it about being present to someone else? Is it about doing something to help another?

4. Whom do I have to forgive in my life? Do I have to forgive myself, first? Who others should be on my list?

5. Charitable works: Do I volunteer in my community to help the lonely, the displaced, the suffering?

6. What is the first commandment and what is the second commandment?

7. How have I lived the second commandment?

Scripture or Quote

Pure love ... knows that only one thing is needed to please God: to do even the smallest things out of great love - love, and always love.
♥ St. Faustina

Our Lord loves you and loves you tenderly; and if He does not let you feel the sweetness of His love, it is to make you more humble and abject in your own eyes.
♥ St. Pio of Pietrelcino

Everything comes from love, all is ordained for the salvation of man, God does nothing without this goal in mind.
♥ St. Catherine of Siena

Healing Prayer

Dear Lord,

Sometimes it's hard for me to show love, and show compassion towards myself or to others. Teach me how to love myself generously as a child of God, and help me to love you more. Help me when I become self-involved, or selfish, and help me when I am incapable of showing acts of love because of the way I grew up, or because I have been hurt. Show me your compassionate heart and the true meaning of sacrifice for _____.

Amen.

Suggested Books and Resources to Help You

🔖 *Four loves.* C.S. Lewis

Notes

_____

_____

_____

_____

_____

_____

_____

_____

Notes

WONDER: *A feeling of surprise mingled with admiration, caused by something beautiful, unexpected, unfamiliar, or inexplicable. awe, admiration, wonderment, fascination; More surprise, astonishment, stupefaction, amazement*

What is Wonder?

If you have visited the Grand Canyon, what emotions did it leave you with? Did it stir your emotions, fill you with awe, leave you with a quiet reverence? Most visitors say something like that. The Grand Canyon lifts most people up into its own Beauty.

We are suddenly surprised by the scale of it all, the grandeur, the magnificence of it, the sheer beauty of this thing that now holds us motionless. It is suddenly too much for us. It suddenly takes us beyond the surface of our little lives. It suddenly plunges us into the Heart of Mystery. It changes your outlook. It touches your soul. Perhaps you found out then that there is more to this world, than tiny little you, and your tiny little concerns.

For most of us, *wonder* is an emotion that grabs us. We are the presence of something outside ourselves: a dazzling sunset; an ocean in a storm; a mountain view that won't stop; a painting that does stop ... you, in your tracks; a movement of a symphony washing over you;

an innocent child-at-play.

One of our favorite landscapes is located just south of Siena in Italy, Tuscany, with its rolling hills and valleys. It is wide, and beautiful, and filled with undulations, and twisting narrow roads, and vines heavy with grapes, and wheat, and towering cypress trees. The first time, I stood on a hill, and looked down onto the vast pastoral landscape, it took my breath away. It made me realize how much God loves beauty and how much he wants us to appreciate the beauty He has made.

What does it look like?

During the journey a dangerous storm overtakes the boat the disciples are in, and they begin to wonder where God is. Jesus then comes walking on the water, and the disciples fear they are seeing a ghost. Jesus calls to them saying "Be not afraid. Take Courage. It is I."

Peter then says "if it is really you, tell me to walk on the water." "Come," Jesus says. Peter climbs out of the boat and begins to walk on the water to Jesus. But as soon as he feels the wind, and sees the waves, he takes his eyes off Jesus, and he begins to sink. Jesus takes Peter by the hand, and they are in the boat, and the storm is no more.

If any of you have ever experienced standing on the shore while a storm is moving in, you might recall the anxiety that swept over you when the wind started to pick up and hit you in the face, and the crests of each wave started to get higher and higher, and the spray spread, and the spray splashed. A storm at sea is a fearsome thing even on shore. In a little boat, it is immeasurably more: vastly unpredictable and dangerous at every moment.

The disciples must have been very surprised, at what they saw, gripped by *wonder* even. Baffled too by the sudden disappearance of wind and wave. *"Truly you are the Son of God,"* they said (Mathew 14:22-33). They could say no more.

Another story also gives us the feeling of Wonder. Mary was filled with wonder (awe) when the Angel of the Lord appeared before her and proclaimed, *"Hail, Mary, full of Grace. The Lord is with you. Blessed are you among women."* (Luke 1:28)

Look all through the Bible, from beginning to end, and you will find that Wonder describes our relationship with Jesus. What does that relationship look like? He looks at us with eyes filled with love. Do you think of him in your daily lives with love? Or are your day to day activities taking you further from a close relationship with Him? Do you treat him like a friend and want to know more about him through the bible, through conversation with your friends, Does He surprise you each day in the things that you see?

He thought of each of us before there ever was a world. He created each of us in his own image. Unless you wonder at this, you are not seeing yourself as God sees you. Do you? See yourself in that way?

Scripture or Quote

Through our lives, the Lord continues to affirm and encourage us.

I praise you, for I am fearfully and wonderfully made. Wonderful are your works; my soul knows it very well.
♥ Psalm 139:14

Then the cherubim lifted up their wings with the wheels beside them, and the glory of the God of Israel hovered over them.
♥ Ezekiel11:22

The tree that is beside the running water is fresher and gives more fruit.
♥ St. Theresa of Avila

Questions to Ask Yourself:

1. Do I see myself as God's pearl of great price? No/Yes Why?

2. When did I realize that God loved me? What is my story?

3. When did I realize that I loved God, Jesus, Our Lady?

4. Questions 4 – 9 will help you to see yourself as a Wonder to yourself and to all of us and to help you to realize that God

has set each of us apart and sees you as special. What is your favorite colour?

5. What is my favorite movie?

6. What is my favorite landscape?

7. Did I see anything interesting today that grabbed me?

8. What would I say is unique about me?

9. What is my favorite king of comfort food?

Healing Prayer

Dear Jesus

Help me to appreciate the wonder that I am, with all my strengths and weaknesses. Let me grow in your love and see myself as you see me, as one worthy of love. Let me know myself, through your eyes, and help me to be renewed each day with the eyes of a child. I want to notice you Lord in all the things that I see, hear, feel, taste, and smell. Let me know the wonder of you presence in each moment.

Amen

Suggested Books and Resources to Help You

🔖 *Seeking Spiritual Direction: How to Grow the Divine Life Within.*
    Father Thomas Dubay.

🔖 *Finding God's Will For You*
    St. Francis de Sales.

🔖 *In the School of the Holy Spirit.*
    Father Jacques Philippe

Notes

_____

_____

_____

_____

_____

_____

_____

_____

Notes

I praise you because I am fearfully and wonderfully made. Wonderful are your works. I know full well.

Psalm 139:14

The title of our ministry,
Grace that Reigns is all about
God's grace present and
working in our lives.

What is Grace?

**Grace is about the
relationship between God
and us.** He invites
Us into his home. He adopts
us as his own daughters and sons.
He shares his own divine life with us. Grace is always a gift,
something that we do not deserve. Gift, it was; and Gift, it is, and Gift,
it always will be.

In the Old Testament, the word for God's Grace is **Hesed**. That
Hebrew word means the loving-kindness God shows his chosen
people, and the grateful love his chosen people show him.

In the New Testament, the word for God's grace is **Charis**. That Greek
word means the love of God that created us, and the love of God that
redeemed us. When he looks upon us with that love, he changes us
in the very core of who we are. This change makes us like his Son:
we are *conformed to Christ*, we say, we take on his very form. This is
called Sanctifying Grace: it sanctifies us; it makes us holy, like the
Lord himself. And this grace stays with us permanently, unless we sin
seriously.

But he does not stop there. In Baptism, he also gives us the Grace of
the Theological Virtues: Faith, Hope, and Charity, to repair our minds

and wills broken by sin. In Baptism, he also gives us the Grace of the Cardinal Virtues: Prudence, Fortitude, Temperance, and Justice, to repair slowly the chaos caused by sin. In Baptism, he also gives us The Grace of the Gifts of the Holy Spirit: these make us ready to receive the Spirit's guidance back to the wholeness we lost in sin. They are wisdom, understanding, counsel, fortitude, knowledge, piety, and fear of the Lord.

And he does not stop there. He also gives us what is called Actual Grace. This is the *Grace of the Moment*: a passing, a temporary, help to see and to do what the Lord wants us to do here and now ... to do his will.

For example, when we need to give a presentation for our religious education class, and we are frightened to speak in public, we might ask for the grace of courage and strength in that moment, so that we can give the speech. Another grace we might like to receive is the grace of endurance, faith or patience when we face a financial challenge and we know that we don't have the human strength to believe that we can make ends meet to last the month.

Grace is a Gift, something we do not deserve, but we can always ask the Lord for his help-that-is-beyond-us, and beyond what we can handle at the moment. We can always ask the Lord for his Grace.

What does it look like?

The receiving of Grace looks like the sunflower's face following the face of the sun as it moves across the sky from east to west. So too do our faces need to follow the Lord in this way. It is made easier for us, of course.

How? Because we are made from love, and God is Love, and that magnetic pull of Love acts the same in each of us. God looks at us with loving eyes and gives us grace abundantly to continue on in our journeys.

Scripture or Quote

My grace is sufficient for thee: for my strength is made perfect in weakness.
♥ 2 Corinthians (12:9)

Grace is nothing else but a certain beginning of glory in us.
♥ St Thomas Aquinas

God opposes the proud but gives Grace to the humble.
♥ 1 Peter (5:5)

Healing Prayer

Dear Lord,

Fill me with your graces of wisdom, knowledge, patience, humility, selflessness, strength, courage, and temperance as I continue to improve or build my faith in you. Help me to trust in you so that I can resist temptation. Teach me to be patient and bear all the trials of suffering or failure that may come to me today. Please give me the grace to know how to approach and encounter others with your love.

Guide me and help me to keep the doors of my heart open to your love, in good times and in bad.

Amen.

Suggested Books and Resources to Help You

🔖 *The Meaning of Grace*
   Charles Cardinal Journet

🔖 *Amazing Grace for the Catholic Heart: 101 Stories of Faith, Hope, Inspiration & Humor*
   Jeff Cavins

Notes

_____

_____

_____

_____

_____

_____

_____

Notes

The basic forms or types of prayer are: **Repentance; Adoration; Petition; and Thanksgiving.** Think of the word **RAPT** as an aid to remembering.

In the Catholic Church, **prayer** is "the raising of one's mind and heart to God," in repentance, in adoration, and in thanksgiving, and also in petition, for all the

spiritual and temporal things we need.

The *Catechism* clearly defines prayer as a "vital and personal relationship with the living and true God" (CCC, no. 2558).

Healing comes when we allow the Lord into our lives, when we allow him to draw close to us, when we allow him to change u. The way we do that is to li t up our minds and hearts to him. And that simple *lifting-up* is Prayer.

Q: How do I begin?

Prayer is easy:
All you have to do is ... **STOP, LOOK, LISTEN.**

Whatever it is that you are so terribly busy with, you need to stop, to put it aside. You need to look for where the Lord is to be found. Where is the Lord to be found? Of course, we know that God is all around us. But, we can also become immediately aware of his presence, by stopping and then, acknowledging Him. This could lead to prayer.

What does the STOP look like?

I am driving in my car and my mind is busy with my life and my duties and problems. I can live with these thoughts, but if I make a decision to turn my mind off for an instant and acknowledge that God is present in my car, and in my heart, I can stay in my pause.. This is the STOP. Now I can pray theses words. *"God, I just want to say hello. I love you. Please guide me."* That is the beginning of my prayer.

What is the LOOK?

How do you continue to pray? Here is an easy way to do that. Look at the Word of God, the Readings of each day's Mass. God always has something to say to you today, that he did not say yesterday, and that he will not say tomorrow. He speaks just to you in those Readings.

Look also at the persons, places, things, and events around you each day. He speaks to you in those things each day. He speaks to you in the Bible as a privileged place, to be sure, but he also speaks to you in the events of your day. We find it harder to hear what he has to say in events, but what he says in them is usually very important for us to hear.

Then LISTEN. What is the Listen?

As you get better at this in practice, he will come closer and closer to you, with his dissolving, healing, presence. Your praying will go beyond mere words. You will find yourself thinking more about God, and what he has in mind for you. And your thinking will go beyond mere concepts. No word of ours will give us the Real God. No thought of ours will give us the Real God. You will find yourself simply gazing at the Tabernacle, say, simply resting in his presence.

Q: What does Prayer look like?

That *Resting* is where it will end. But there are three basic forms of prayer that you should know.

1. Vocal Prayer

Vocal Prayer is prayer through audible words. It is most important that we attend to the words we are saying, because the heart should be present to God. Because it is external and so thoroughly human, vocal prayer is the form of prayer most readily accessible to groups. (Catechism of the Catholic Church, 2700 and 2704) It is also a prayer that we never outgrow.

2. Meditation

Meditation is turning our thoughts to God. It is thinking about God. It is a quest to know more and more about him, and how we should live his supernatural life. We meditate when we think about the Readings of the Mass. We meditate when we think about the qualities of God. We meditate when we think about how the Saints live their Christian lives. If you allow yourself to sit quietly and you close your eyes, it can help you to become more aware of your sense.

3. Contemplation

It is a gaze of faith, fixed on Jesus. "I don't do anything. I don't say anything. I just look at him, and he just looks at me" as an old peasant told St. John Vianney when he asked the man what he did before the Tabernacle.. (CCC no.2715)

What the mouth cannot say, and the mind cannot think, the heart can love, and rest in, in silence. What does contemplation look like? To me, it looks like two people who are in love and you catch them just gazing at each other, in each others' presence. Nothing needs to be said. I can feel them almost communicating silently to each other. They seem to be in touch each other. Contemplation is silently falling in love with Jesus and feeling thankful to be in His presence and expressing gratitude for his generosity.

Prayer is always required to ensure that your personal relationship/ friendship with Christ keeps growing.

4. Setting the Mood for Prayer

All the way through primary school, I shared a bedroom with my sister. We shared a lamp, we shared our books, we shared our closet space, and we even shared our pet bees and bugs. We shared almost everything. But the one thing that we did not share was our prayer corner. Those corners were our own – and they were special to us.

Mine had a little picture of Jesus pasted on the wall, with a number of glow in the dark stickers of candles and animals and hearts surrounding the picture. I even constructed a little shelf made of cardboard and taped it on two corners so that I could place my rosary there. The fact was, it was mine, and it was a special place where I could talk to Jesus before I went to sleep and where I could say good morning to him, when I woke up. Little did I know, but it was already helping me to form a good prayerful habit.

Questions to Ask Yourself:

1. Do I create a quiet place to pray that is my own and conducive to prayer? A comfy chair, candle, pictures of Jesus, Our Lady, the Saints, etc. Do I have a Bible there to hear the Word of God? Is my Rosary there? Do I turn off my smartphone for the duration of my prayer? Do my family members know not to interrupt you when you are there?

2. Have I cultivated a habit of prayer? Do I take time out for alone time with God?

3. Do I know what times of the day you can pray most effectively?

4. Of the three forms of prayer, which of the three am I most comfortable with at this time? Do I talk more, do I think more, or do I rest with the Lord more?

5. Do I write my thoughts and reflections in a journal? It is always good to review our prayer briefly when we finish.

6. Do I have a prayer partner with whom I can share?

7. Do I truly believe that God is listening to me and that He will answer my prayers, in His way, if not in my own?

Scripture or Quote

For me, prayer is a surge of the heart; it is a simple look turned toward heaven, it is a cry of recognition and of love, embracing both trial and joy. Contemplative prayer [oracion mental] is nothing else than a close sharing between friends; it means taking time frequently to be alone with him who we know loves us.
♥ St. Therese of Lisieux

Healing Prayer

Dear Jesus,

Please give me the desire to know you more in prayer, and to be strengthened in my will to depend only on you. Open my heart to your Spirit of truth and keep me close to you as I continue on my daily journey. Guide me so that my prayer life will become habitual, and bless all of my family and friends around me so that they too may be uplifted by your grace.

Amen.

Suggested Books and Resources to Help You

🔖 *Practice of the Presence of God*
    Brother Lawrence of the Resurrection

🔖 *The Art of Praying*
    Romano Guardini

🔖 *When the Well Runs Dry*
    Thomas Green, SJ

🔖 *Come, Be My Light*
    Mother Theresa

Notes

_____

_____

_____

_____

_____

_____

_____

_____

Notes

During our retreats, we speak about the ups and downs in your journey of prayer.

We do this because we know that the long road from conversion to heaven is filled with spiritual challenges. Those times when you feel up to praying is called a time of Consolation. Those times when you do not feel up to praying is called a time of Desolation.

Q: What is Spiritual Consolation?

A: It is a sense of *lightness*, of being *up*, of being *uplifted*, of being energized. It is a sense of being filled with the presence of God. It varies in intensity, and in how long it lasts. And it always has a direct relationship to our friendship with God: it does its best to deepen that friendship.

Some Characteristics of Consolation:

It directs our focus outside and beyond ourselves, and it makes us more sensitive to God.

- It makes us more desirous of being led by God himself. We begin to hunger for that daily guidance.

- It puts order in all our relationships: we begin to love all persons and things in God. Many of our tangles are untangled, then. And we feel a new energy for a life with God.

What is Spiritual Desolation?

Spiritual Desolation is a feeling of heaviness, of darkness, of dryness, and of confusion when we begin to pray. Where Consolation is the *Up*, Desolation is the *Down*. During these times, there is no excitement or pleasure at the thought of spiritual things. When we try to pray, we see nothing, and we feel nothing. It saps our energy. As time goes on, confusion, doubts and anxieties grow deep within our hearts and minds. It always has a direct relationship to our friendship with God: it does its best to destroy that friendship.

Some Characteristics of Desolation

- Not everyone experiences a mind blowing conversion experience. For some of us, it is a slow steady progress.

- One of the characteristics of desolation is that it directs our focus inside, on ourselves, because it leaves us feeling abandoned. We have no taste for God, no energy for God.

- Being caught up in spiritual desolation leads you to believe that the dryness you feel is all your fault; that you never had a real relationship with God in the first place; that you are just flat no good.

- It wreaks havoc in your relationships: the normal tangles become more tangled. And we have no energy for trying to untangle impossible

Nobody really wants to talk about Sin today.

We have largely lost our sense of sin. Nothing that happens to us is our fault. There is always someone else to blame. We are poor, mistreated, victims. The world owes us. God owes us. We no longer know how to say: *I did it. It was my mistake. It was my fault.* We no longer know how to pray: *Lord, Have Mercy on me, a sinner.*

Our first parents sinned, and were alienated from God, and from one another, and from the world around them. How could their children, born into such a radical alienation, fail to be affected by it. How could it not affect the way they feel about things, the way they see things, the way they judge things? It is no wonder that siblings fight for attention and love. And it is no wonder that self-centered parents are so poor at giving them either one. Adam and Ever said *Thanks, God*: for this lovely garden, for this beautiful woman, for this strong man.

Thanks, but no thanks. We'll take it from here. We'd rather do it our way. The world the way he made it, with its complex and subtle connections, was not to their liking. They would rather remake it in their own image and likeness.

And so, sin, alienation, chaos: inside them, and outside them. Sin darkened their minds, and confused their thoughts and decisions. Sin set up the unending struggle between selfishness and selflessness.

Sin set loose what we came to know as the *Seven Deadly Sins*, pride, greed, lust, envy, gluttony, wrath, and sloth (These are not actual sins, so much, as inclinations, tendencies, weaknesses we have that lead us into sin). You'd think we would learn. But so long as we insist on doing it our way, we never will.

Confession: The thing to remember about Sin is that Jesus died for our sins and that he loves us even if we do sin. If we sin, and we are contrite in heart, we can seek forgiveness through the sacrament of Confession. When we walk out of the Confessional, we are free. Jesus extends his mercy to us in every time of need.

Q: What does it look like?

Sin is any movement away from God. To counter it, confession, repentance, good works are needed to help bring God's healing grace into your life.

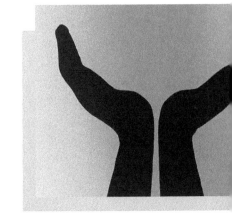

Conversion simply is a change that turns our minds and hearts upside down. The Holy Spirit works this change through the Grace won by

Jesus Christ in his death and resurrection. This Good News is ours for the asking. But remember that Jesus said: *the Kingdom is near, REPENT, and believe this Good News.*

We have to see our sins for what they are, accept responsibility for them, and ask for God's forgiveness of them, in the way he chose to give us that forgiveness.

Questions to Ask Yourself:

1. When was the last time I explored, evaluated, and considered my sins?

2. When was the last time I knew I was supposed to do good, but decided not to do it?

3. When was the last time I was self-righteous, or self centered? When I blamed everybody but yourself? When I played the victim?

4. When was the last time I willfully ignored God's commandments?

5. When was the last time I went to Confession or countered my sin with acts of charity?

6. When was the last time I apologized to someone?

Scripture or Quote

Search me, O God, and know my heart! Try me and know my thoughts!
♥ Psalm (139:23)

*My little children, I am writing these things to you so that you may not sin.
But if anyone does sin, we have an advocate with the Father, Jesus Christ the
righteous.*
♥ 1 John (2:1)

*The saints, too, had wandering minds. The saints, too, had constantly to recall
their constantly wandering mind-child home. They became saints because they
continued to go after the little wanderer, like the Good Shepherd.*
♥ Peter Kreeft

Healing Prayer

Dear Lord,

Help me to draw closer to you, and to be open to your spirit of
truth. Enlighten my conscience so that I may see how to live more
honestly. Strengthen my will, and my heart, so that I may find the
strength to resist and overcome temptation. Help me to be gentler to
myself as I continue to learn about your gift of mercy. Help me
not to despair, but to have the humility to be humble of heart to

I know that I am responding to a nudge to ask for the Lord's forgivness. Forgive me and set me free from the sins that bind me.

Amen.

Suggested Books and Resources to Help You

🔖 *Introduction to Moral Theology*
    William E. May

🔖 *People of the Lie*
    M. Scott Peck, MD

🔖 *The Screwtape Letters*
    C.S. Lewis

Notes

_____

_____

_____

_____

_____

_____

Notes

Believe it or not, **WE** are the biggest thing standing in the way of our personal relationship with Christ. Why is that so? Because we often get stuck in a self-concept that prevents us from getting out of self, from branching out and trying new things, and from letting ourselves go in Faith.

Part of our journey will consist of periods of Desolation. During those dark times, our own personal barriers and obstacles begin to surface. That's why Desolation is an integral part of our journey to God: without it we would not come to know these barriers in a way we can do something about them. Some of them are old weaknesses, we have long known. Some of them are hidden tendencies we have never seen clearly.

They all try to do the same thing: to stop us in our tracks from understanding God's love for us, and from pursuing the vocation he has for us.

Barriers or obstacles that hold us back from our personal relationship with God should be addressed with the same kind of dedication and hard work. We have found in our retreats four obstacles that return time after time:

1. **Fear** (and the lack of trust it hides)
2. **Control**
3. **Feeling Unworthy**
4. **Un-forgiveness** (and the resentment it breeds)

When we expose them, and name them, and talk about them, we can finally begin working free from them, and begin coming ever closer to the person God made us to be; that person filled with Wonder.

What does it look like?

Consider the lowly sponge. We use it on our dishes. We use it on our cars. The work of a sponge is to clean. It swallows all that dirt, and, with a squeeze from us, it allows that dirt to flow away.
When you squeeze a sponge, water and all that is it runs out

of its holes. Or it is supposed to. In fact, a squeeze will not normally empty a sponge: deeper inside the holes, dirt might be lodged in those spaces. These are the things that sin hands down to us. They get stuck in our spaces, and over time, they can harden and become obstacles and barriers that inhibit our growth. If we are filled with "stuff," how is God ever going to fill up our holes?

1. Fear / Lack of Trust

Photo Courtesy of Juliana Loh

Fear is an elastic word: it stretches wide to hold oddly-shaped things that seem ill-suited to fit in a single word.

It is the emotional reaction to a threat on your horizon. We fear the evil thing camped on the outskirts of our town. It is not here yet, but we can almost feel it, can almost

hear it breathing destruction.   Most will do one of two things: they
will dissolve in flight, or they will stiffen in fight. We can slip out
the back-door in the dark. Or we can be galvanized into action, by
standing up and preparing to meet the threat.

It is also the spiritual reaction to the Real God himself. *The fear of the
Lord is the beginning of Wisdom*, the Bible said (Proverbs 1:7). The writer
was trying to say something of God's overwhelming Goodness, Love,
and Mercy, and also something of God's unending sense of fairness,
his overpowering Justice.

He will judge the free human creatures he made on how they have
lived, and that will lead to an eternal life with him, or without him:
it will lead to heaven or to hell. But he will also save us, because he is
always ready to forgive when we repent of what we have done. There
is good reason to be lost in wonder at his unexpected, overwhelming,
Mercy. Fear of this kind is more awe than it is *flight or fight*.

Fear of this kind strengthens the gift of Hope that he gave us in our
Baptism. It does so especially when our spirits flag and fail at the
threats around us. Fear (a *filial fear* that is lost in the wonder of God:
the easy, at-home fear of a child with his parents) drives out fear (a
servile fear that quakes before a possible ultimate end, the reality of
Hell: the uneasy fear, panic even, that drives us out the back door into
the night). *Fear drives out fear.*

What does it look like?

Fear can be disguised as worry or anxiety. A friend of mine told me
once, that he would be open to anything the Lord asked of him,
except for being a missionary apostle in a third world country. I asked
him why and he said that he didn't think he could handle the living
conditions and he feared meeting new people who were so different
from him.

At bottom, he felt anxious and knew that this opportunity would over-stretch his faith and soon the worry turned into fear. When a friend of his invited him to go, his feeling of fear thus prevented him from being open to this new possibility and a new adventure.

Worries/Anxiety can lead to Fear

There are different kinds of worries and anxieties that can turn into fear. These fears can become barriers in your journey.

- Worry of not being accepted - or fearing what others think of you can lead to a fear of being abandoned.
- Worry about being perfect, can lead to a fear of starting.
- Worry about being judged, can lead to fear of being rejected.
- Worry of failing can lead to a fear of growing.
- Worry or anxiety about being intimate with others, can lead to a fear of displaying your feelings, and being vulnerable to family or friends.
- Worry of the future can lead to our fears of growing older.
- Worry of not knowing all the answers can lead to your fear of following a call from Jesus.
- Worry and anxiety of growing old can lead to a fear of death
- Not completely trusting in the Lord can cause fears in all areas of your life.

Scripture or Quote

There is no fear in love. But perfect love drives out fear, because fear has to do with punishment. The one who fears is not made perfect in love.
❤ John 1:4-8

Be not afraid, for I am with you. Be not discouraged, for I am your God. I will strengthen you and help you. I will hold you up with my victorious right hand.
❤ Isaiah 41:10

Healing Prayer

Dear Lord,

Please help me to know my fears, and release me from my fears: those that I am aware of, those that feed my anxiety; those so deep inside me that I cannot understand. Fill me with your presence, fill me with courage, strength, and increase in faith and comfort so that I can be released from the fears that I encounter inside of me. Heal my memories from the things that harmed me, fill me with your loving grace, and free me from every bondage of fear. Help me to trust and have hope in you.

Amen

Suggested Books and Resources to Help You

🔖 *The Divine Pity*
   Gerald Vann OP

🔖 *An Introduction to the Devout Life*
   St Francis de Sales

Alleviating Anxiety and Fears

We encourage you to journal about your anxieties and experiences, especially taking into account, the times when your anxiety was due to overwhelming emotion rather than reliance upon facts.

We also encourage you to record the times when the Lord intervened in your life to solve your anxiety or fear through grace or action. Keep a record of those times, because they will help you to trust in God's providence and remind you to trust in Him when you face your fears again.

Notes

_____

_____

_____

_____

_____

_____

Notes

"Peace is what I leave with you; it is my own peace that I give you. I do not give it as the world does. Do not be worried and upset; do not be afraid."

John 14:27

2. Control

Control is a word most of us are very familiar with. Most of us need to have varying levels of control in our lives; some more than others, but a person who is obsessed with the desire to be in control is in effect, " out of control " because he or she is un-free to receive advice, or opinions or help from others."

Sometimes, this trait can get in the way of our communion with God when we become obsessively attached to it. We all know control-freaks, and they come in all sizes, shapes, and hues. Unless they have total control over everything they have, everything they want, everything they will have, they cannot rest easy. They are obsessed with planning for each and every contingency that might occur.

If you have lived with such a person, you know the dreadful consequences of such an attitude. It wrecks families, it wrecks jobs, it wrecks neighborhoods, it wrecks towns, it wrecks governments. Control promises far more than it can ever deliver. Control, too, is a lie.

Go again to *Creation*. The Lord made the world from nothing. He made man from dust, Genesis tells us. And all created things will return to dust. This does not mean that we will cease to exist, but that we will be transformed. No amount of thinking, planning, and executing is going to arrest *this* process.

The thing to do is to **accept** that things are ultimately beyond us.

The thing to do is to **trust in the Lord** who made the *lilies of the field*.

That acceptance is the first step toward healing this unfortunate attitude.

How does it look like?

We have noticed, during times of sharing at our retreats, that people who want to be perceived as being the "busiest," usually have more difficulty letting go of control.

The most difficult thing to adjust to is **losing a sense of control over one's life.** This person finds it hard to let go and let God take care of everything. Not surprisingly, these people find it very difficult to surrender to another person, least of all, to the Holy Spirit.

The fact is, we don't really control our own destiny nor can we exercise absolute control over our own lives in any sense. A person who insists on being in control of his or her future must ask the Lord for the grace to learn how to trust in Him, and the grace to be more humble.

Questions to Ask Yourself:

1. Do I always have answers to questions that are asked?

2. Do I always need to know the outcome of events?

3. Do I perceive that my needs are more important? Or do I consider what the Lord wants for me?

4. Do I dictate my partner's future, or my own future?

5. Do I use the word " I " too much? I want ..., I need ..., I am ....

6. Do I get angry a lot when things don't go my way?

Scripture or Quote

For I know the plans I have for you, declares the Lord, plans for welfare and not for evil, to give you a future and a hope.
♥ Jeremiah 29:11

And now, O Lord, for what do I wait? My hope is in you.
♥ Psalm 39:7

Healing Prayer

Dear Lord,

Help me to see myself as a person you love. Fill me with humility. Love and protect me from projecting my own fears and insecurities onto others. Give me the grace to surrender my actions to you, and to follow in your footsteps. In times of stress, increase my love, faith, and awareness of you and allow me to offer my will to

you. Amen

Suggested Books and Resources to Help You

- 🔖 *True Devotion to Mary: Preparation for Total Consecration*
  Saint Louis de Montfort

- 🔖 *The Gift of Faith*
  Father Tadeusz Dajczer

Notes

_____

_____

_____

_____

_____

_____

_____

_____

Notes

3. Feeling Unworthy

One trait that gets in the way of our communion with God is a sense of our own unworthiness. I do not mean that we need to do away with the virtue of Humility, of course. There is another kind of unworthiness.

Somewhere in our formative years, some of us seem to have picked up the idea that we were not good enough, and that we would never be good enough. Something tricked us into thinking that we were, at bottom, unlovable. This can have devastating consequences for the way we live our lives. It can paralyze us, and stop us from doing anything. It can leave us too timid to risk, too timid to dare.

But if you really understand what creation means, if you really understand what Redemption means, you will see that this sense of unworthiness is a lie. The Father made you out of love, the Son redeemed you out of love, the Spirit who lives in you is Love. You are *worth more than many sparrows* to the members of the Trinity. You are precious to them. You are deeply loved because you are deeply lovable.

How deep is God's love?

Remember the parable of the Good Shepherd, who left the 99 sheep who were healthy and strong, in order to go after the one sheep that was lost and in need. When he found that sheep, he rejoiced!

God loves you so much that he knows that your desire to follow him, to pray, to know him, makes him feel so happy, filled with joy.

God just wants to take delight in you.

Q: What does this look like and how does it affect you?

Each of us, at times, feels insecure and unworthy of God's love. Especially when we failed at a task, or when we feel especially guilty for a sin that we committed. In those times, we can become discouraged and thus feel unworthy of Christ's love.

We are not the only ones who suffer this way and when we do, we can look to St. Paul who is a great example of one who has also experienced discouragement and struggle and feelings of unworthiness, especially on his missionary journeys. During those times, he recognized his weakness, AND, he rejoiced in his weakness. Why? Because it forced him to depend more on God, rather than on his own feelings.

What he said was: *I am well content with these humiliations of mine, with the insults, the hardships, the persecutions, the times of difficulty I undergo for Christ: when I am weakest, then I am strongest of all.* (2 Corinthians 12:10)

Photo Courtesy of Bishop Ronald Gilmore

Questions to Ask Yourself:

1. In the words that we pray, *Lord, I am not worthy to receive you, but only say the word and I shall be healed.* Do I really believe in Christ's promise of healing?

2. What stirrings, memories, words, or emotions caused by

another, plunged you into those feelings of unworthiness? Were you bullied as a child, told that you weren't good enough by your parents, not *taken* seriously by your colleagues?

3. When I recall those memories, as a mature person today, can I counter those feelings that they evoke by concentrating on all my blessings, and achievements?

4. Can I overflow with gratitude for all these? Can I pour myself out in acts of kindness? Can I write these down and add to them?

5. When I am feeling particularly low in your faith life, do I give in to discouragement, or do I make an act of trust, turning away from it, and concentrating on Jesus?

6. Do I help myself by reading the Scriptures, especially the Psalms, or by listening to Christian music, or by talking to a good friend about my struggles with faith?

7. Do I pray to be filled with God's mercy and love, so that it can counter my feeling of discouragement and unworthiness?

8. Do I ask for the Grace to put all of my faith and trust in the Lord?

9. Do I smile, and tell Satan to stop playing mind games with me when I am feeling discouraged?

10. Do you find it easy or hard to forgive myself?

11. Do I get angry a lot when things don't go my way?

Scripture or Quote

Jesus revealed to St. Margaret Mary that even if all the sins of the world were on her soul, compared to his burning love for her, they would be like a drop of water thrown into a blazing furnace.

Lord, I am not worthy to receive you, but only say the word and I shall be healed.

God shows his love for us in that while we were still sinners,
Christ died for us
♥ Romans 5:8

Healing Prayer

Dear Lord,

You know how unworthy I feel to ask for your help. Give me the strength to forget about myself and see myself as a beautiful person, worthy of love. I am in your hands and they are very good and gently hands. Let me trust in you whole-heartedly and help me to recognize how much you love me, even with all of my feelings of insecurity and imperfections. I am worthy because I am me. **Help me to believe in me.**

Amen.

Suggested Books and Resources to Help You

- *Abandonment to Divine Providence*
  Jean-Pierre de Caussade

- *Understanding "Our Father"*
  Scott Hahn

Notes

_____

_____

_____

_____

_____

_____

_____

_____

_____

_____

_____

Notes

The Light Shines in the Darkness, but the darkness did not comprehend it.

John 1:5

Who hasn't been hurt by the actions or words of another? Perhaps a parent constantly criticized you while growing up, a colleague sabotaged a project, or your classmates made fun of you. Or maybe you've had a traumatic experience, such as being physically or

emotionally abused by someone close to you. These wounds can leave you with lasting feelings of anger and bitterness — even with a desire for revenge.

The only line in the Lord's Prayer that has a condition attached is the

line about forgiveness. *Forgive us our trespasses* **AS** *we forgive those who trespass against us.* There is a world of weight in the two letters of that tiny word. We will be forgiven to the degree that we forgive: no *ifs*, or *ands*, or *buts* about it.

But this is too hard, you say. *But this is not the way the world works*, you say. *But you don't really know what she did to me*, you say. *But you don't really know how he hurt me, you say. I will not forgive*, you say. I'll store it up, keep it inside, feed it some fuel, like some of those toxic coal fires deep in the earth that never go out. That's how a bitter, poisonous, resentment is born.

When you do this, you are condemning yourself to a prison of your own making. Sometimes it feels good to hate and seek revenge. But when you do that, you thus build bars of hate around yourself. This will take away your peace of mind, this will damage a relationship once dear to you, this will jeopardize your eternal soul. You are a sad spectacle in the prison you made. Its only saving feature is that you did not know how to give it a lock.

It is in your power to open the door, and at any time. Forgive us, as we forgive others. Ask for his healing, with sincerity, and he will grant it to you.

What does this look like and how does it affect you?

There are times when others hurt us, and resentment creeps in. Do you let that feeling fester, and allow un-forgiveness to creep in too? When we don't forgive, bitterness and resentment can set it. This can have a great affect on the way we view ourselves, our lives of faith and our relationship with God. Bitterness and resentment is like a black hole that draws everything into itself, including you.

A common example can be found in the action of divorce. It can be very a very messy experience for both parties, filled with arguments, anxiety, bitterness, resentment, jealousy and pain. At times, it can take years to resolve and for forgiveness to occur. During that time, people either get angry, or withdraw.

Keeping all that negative feeling bottled up can do terrible things to your physical, mental, and spiritual health. Keeping anger and resentment inside for prolonged periods of time becomes corrosive and will prevent God's healing grace from getting through to us. Thank God we have the Sacrament of Confession.

If you are unable to forgive, you might:

- Bring anger and bitterness into every other relationship
- Become so wrapped up in the wrong that you can't enjoy the moment.
- Become depressed or anxious.
- Allow the way you live to be at odds with your spiritual beliefs.

- Lose valuable and enriching connections with others.
- Think of forgiveness, and how it can change your life by bringing you peace, happiness, and emotional and spiritual healing.

Questions to Ask Yourself:

1. **Think about the last time you were hurt by someone.**
   Do I still bear a grudge against that person? What level of anger do I have for this person? Has it turned to bitterness or dreams of revenge?

2. Have I asked for God's Grace to help myself to forgive my offender, or have I willfully decided to live with the feelings?

3. How long ago has it been since I asked the Lord for forgiveness, for my own actions against others?

4. Is my feeling of anger a result of resentment or un-forgiveness?

5. How long generally, does it take me to forgive someone?

Scripture or Quote

When they hurled their insults at him, he did not retaliate; when he suffered, he made no threats. Instead, he entrusted himself to him who judges justly.
♥ 1 Peter 2:23

Jesus said, Father, forgive them, for they do know not what they do...
♥ Luke: 23-34

What causes fights and quarrels among you? Don't they come from your desires that battle within you? You desire but do not have, so you kill. You covet but you cannot get what you want, so you quarrel and fight. You do not have because you do not ask God.
♥ James 4:1-2

Get rid of all bitterness.
♥ Ephesians 4:31

Healing Prayer

Ask God to cleanse your memory. Instead of remembering with malice, injustice, and hurt, remember with forgiveness. Then go one step further and ask God to forgive your offender. By forgiving and then asking God to forgive your offender, you release God to bless you and the other person.

Dear Jesus,

Please help me because I know that I've held resentment and bitterness against _____. I confess this as a sin and ask you to for your mercy. Please help me to forgive myself, and _____ also. When temptation strikes me, give me your grace not to hold any more resentments, but help me to forgive this person. I want to be at peace and I want to be free of this burden.

Amen.

Suggested Books and Resources to Help You

📖 *Facing Forgiveness: A Catholic's Guide to Letting Go of Anger and Welcoming Reconciliation*
Gregory Aymond, Carroll Julio, and Loughland Sofield

Here is a list of some wickedly high speed bumps you might run into on your journey of faith.

- ☐ Anger
- ☐ Addiction
- ☐ Anxiety
- ☐ Argumentativeness
- ☐ Boredom
- ☐ Broken friendships
- ☐ Business difficulties
- ☐ Conception and pregnancy difficulties
- ☐ Concern for departed loved ones
- ☐ Criticism
- ☐ Depression
- ☐ Distractions during prayer
- ☐ Distrust in God
- ☐ Doubts
- ☐ Drunkenness
- ☐ Envy
- ☐ Failure
- ☐ False accusations
- ☐ Family difficulties
- ☐ Financial difficulties
- ☐ Gloominess
- ☐ Gluttony
- ☐ Gossip
- ☐ Greed
- ☐ Grief
- ☐ Guilt
- ☐ Illness
- ☐ Impatience
- ☐ Irritations
- ☐ Irreligious children
- ☐ Judgmental bent
- ☐ Loneliness
- ☐ Lust
- ☐ Marital problems
- ☐ Old age
- ☐ Pride
- ☐ Self-indulgence
- ☐ Spiritual dryness
- ☐ Tardiness
- ☐ Temptations
- ☐ Timidity and/or aggressiveness
- ☐ Uncertainty
- ☐ Unforgiveness
- ☐ Unpopularity

YOU ARE NOT ALONE!

Whatever you are struggling with, you are not alone: there's a Saint who is not only praying for you before the throne of God, but who also went through the same thing you're going through. In Saintly Solutions, Fr. Joseph Esper introduces you to over 350 saints who suffered in ways that you and I suffer every day, and who will bring you also to peace.

We recommend the following book, from which the list on the previous page was taken.

Saintly Solutions to Life's Common Problems
Father Joseph M. Esper

We have now helped you identify the biases, the bumps, and the roadblocks on your journey. We have helped you to understand that you are not alone in it. These are good things. But to keep strengthened in faith, we now want to pray healing prayers for you.

Q: What is the Church's position on healing?

A: Jesus came to earth to preach, teach, and to heal. When you look closely at them, those three things, preaching, teaching and healing are almost synonymous.

We can see that in Matthew's gospel when he summarizes: *"And Jesus went about all Galilee, teaching in their synagogues, and preaching the gospel of the kingdom, and healing all manner of sickness and all manner of disease among the people"* Matt. (4:23)

Matthew then emphasizes the fact that Jesus did Heal.

"And his fame went throughout all Syria: and they brought unto him all sick people that were taken with divers diseases and torments, and those which were possessed with devils, and those which were lunatic, and those that had the palsy; and he healed them" (Matt. 4:24)

Finally, at the Great Commission, which is known as the final direction given by Jesus, the very last thing that He tells His apostles is for all of them to **save, heal, deliver, and disciple.**

"In My name they will cast out demons; they will speak with new tongues; they will take up serpents; and if they drink anything deadly, it will by no means

hurt them; they will lay hands on the sick, and they will recover. " Mark (16:15-18)

Q: How does Grace that Reigns further help you on your journey of healing?

While healing occurs at all Masses, through the consecration of the body and blood, (the Sacrifice of Calvary, along with the Resurrection, here is the source of every healing) our ministry has also been very effective at helping people heal from roadblocks, and obstacles to a living faith.

During our retreats and missions, Jacqueline Loh uses the charisms of healing and the discernment of spirits, gifts of the Holy Spirit, in praying with people. Bishop Ronald Gilmore, on the other hand, uses the gifts of priestly office in praying with people, during the Eucharist, Confession, and the other Sacraments.

We make ourselves available for individual prayer and for the Sacrament of Confession. We also make time available for adoration of the Eucharistic Body of the Lord, and quiet prayer in his presence.

We ask you to bring your own problems and obstacles to that Eucharistic Adoration. He, again, is the source of all healing. Surrender to him the very areas most in need of his presence and power.

Q: What are the various forms of healing?

You can receive a Physical, or a Mental, or an Emotional, or a Spiritual healing, and, not infrequently, some combination of these.

Physical healing involves something as small as a sprained toe up to something as dramatic as the healing of cancer.

Mental healing involves things of the mind, like deep-rooted sinful habits, addictions, and obsessions.

Emotional healing involves the healing of the heart, like wounds from childhood, wounds from adolescence, heartbreak, and deep discouragement.

Spiritual healing involves things of the Spirit, your personal relationship with Jesus of Nazareth. The Seven Deadly Sins, singly and together, war against that relationship. Spiritual healing is the most important type of healing that helps you cope with those deadly tendencies, and it frees you from them...

Healing Prayer for your Continuing Journey

As you begin to name your own habits, and tendencies, and obstacles, and barriers, do not wallow in fear of them. Simply ask the Lord to fill your every dimension with his healing love. Try to be gentle with yourself, and allow Him to do the work you need..

We will help you to pray for endurance, and strength in facing your battles. We will also pray for protection from the enemy. Finally, we will pray for the Lord's own gift of Consolation, which will lift you up and give you peace.

Dear Jesus,

Heal my heart from any feelings of vulnerability, pain, or embarrassment as I worked through the contents of this retreat, and examined my soul. Fill the holes in my heart with the grace of acceptance, as I ask you to make me whole again. Allow me to see myself as you see me, and to love myself as you love me. Protect me from the spirits that annoy me and war against me. Let me know again that I am your adopted child, at home in your home, at home in your heart, and at home on your lap.

Amen

Photo Courtesy of Ryle Anthony Brual

We want you to become aware that you are, in Christ, more than the sum of all of your parts. We want you to know that your weaknesses, and tendencies, and sins do not define you. The Lord allows them to bedevil you so that you may know them, and may learn to resist them.

You have now named your major barriers, and have allowed God to transform your heart through healing prayer or through Confession. What comes next? You might want to build up your own confidence in the person you are becoming, and the God who is making you so.

At the start of this retreat, we asked what makes you *Unique*. Yes you are unique and you are now more than ever aware that God LOVES YOU!! God's love for you is so overflowing. Since **the nature of Love always extends outwards**, how will you build up your family, friends and Church community around you? Take another step now. Let's uncover your talents.

Q: What are your talents?

Talents are natural aptitudes or skills: facility, gift, knack, touch, ability, touch, capacity that we excel in. Examples of talents include: singing, dancing, writing poetry, acting, working with horses, riding.

What do I have a natural aptitude for?

Q: What are your charisms?

These are gifts of God give to you for the sake of others. For information on these, please go the **Siena Institute** at *www.Siena.org*. You will find there much more information about talents, gifts, and charisms there.

What is my Next Step?   GIVE THANKS, PRAISE GOD.

This retreat was a retreat to open your mind and heart to the wonder of you, and for the wonder of your journey with God.

Thank you for hosting a Grace that Reigns Event and most especially, for your lively participation in these days.

Sing a new song to the Lord. It will take a new song, your own song, to praise the Lord for all the wonders he created for us. Praise him most of all, for being THE source of Wonder to us.

What next?

Take time to review this material, soak it in, pray on it. Go back to it, reflect on the questions and answer some of the questions again. Bring it to your prayer groups. Share your experiences. Ask questions, and ask the Lord to continue to reveal his path to you. Share your experiences about our retreats or about this spiritual book.

Philip Lawler once said, *In more than thirty years as a journalist covering Catholicism, I have found that the most exciting signs of vigorous life in the Church often comes from unexpected directions.*

"Far from the limelight, prayerful Catholic individuals, without formal credentials and without financial support, working alone, or in small groups, they quietly work wonders."

Please also remember to pray for Bishop Gilmore and Jacqueline Loh at *Grace that Reigns*: that they might continue to bring this ministry of Wonder and Healing to priests and people of many dioceses.

Notes

_____

_____

_____

_____

_____

_____

_____

_____

_____

_____

_____

_____

The Exodus Story is a story of Wonder and Awe.

The Hebrew children went down into Egypt in order to survive. There they were turned into slaves. But the Lord heard their cry for help. He sent them mighty Moses. Against all odds, he led his people out into the desert, and then, he led them toward the Promised Land. Their adventure has never ceased to inspire our own adventure.

Through this retreat, we helped you explore what it means to be caught in circumstances you cannot control. You know what it meant to be in the grip of burdensome things. You know what it meant to be a slave. You know how the journey felt. If we have helped free you from many things ... personal situations, fears, habits, burdens ... then this Retreat has been a success.

The Lord made us free, in his own image and likeness.

At times, it seems that we make a mess of the freedom he gives us. If we come to our senses, like the Prodigal Son, we will be able to give him the mess of our lives, and ask Him to free us yet again.

He is already close to us: he makes his home in us. If we turn our wandering attention back to him, he

will heal us, and he will set us free. From that moment, even though we are less than half-healed, we will know Joy, and delight, in the presence of the Lord.

Your Journey began in Wonder, It continues in Wonder, and It will end in Wonder. A Garden re-found. A Paradise reclaimed. Heaven. Blessed Wonder.

After participating in our retreats/workshops, people have told us that they have found relief in being offered a chance to re-discover their own personal issues with guidance. They have also shared that it has been a much better experience to explore these topics with other like-minded people of faith.

In understanding what the church says about these topics, and about healing in general, many have also confided that they gained a better appreciation and confidence in themselves as *"Pearls of Great Price."*

People have also shared that they were also able to move forward on their journey of faith with a new sense of freedom, joy, and relief after exploring their personal obstacles.

"When all the instrumentalists of an orchestra come together to play, music and magic happens." (Jacqueline Loh)

The kingdom of heaven is like a merchant seeking beautiful pearls, who, when he had found one pearl of great price, went and sold all that he had and bought it.

Matt 13:45-46

Who are we?

An unlikely and providential partnership formed in 2003 when Bishop Ronald Gilmore invited Jacqueline Loh to Dodge City to pray for a priest who was in desperate need for prayers and for healing.

Jacqueline then invited Bishop Gilmore to join her at Grace that Reigns in 2012 and since then, this ministry has matured and grown and God's grace has been brought to many in Canada and in the United States. *God is so good and so surprising!*

Mission Statement

1. Renewing a Sense of Wonder for your love & relationship with Jesus and for your own goodness, by sharing our teachings, stories, and inspiring testimonies

2. Identifying and healing misconceptions, roadblocks, stereotypes, and hidden barriers that affect our ability to see ourselves as Unique, Loved, and a Pearl of Great Price

3. Promoting Eucharistic adoration and Confession and healing prayers to Pastors and Parishes

4. Providing Opportunities for God's Divine Supernatural Healing Grace to transform lives

Offering

Retreats, spiritual direction, and missions to Clergy and Parishes.

Jacqueline Loh

... comes from the Archdiocese of Vancouver, Canada. She is the founder of *Grace that Reigns*, in Canada and in the United States. She was working happily as a Landscape Architect when God asked her to serve Him. She was hesitant to leave her career, but after praying, she found that she could help more people by founding this retreat ministry. She speaks of God's love for us in a manner that celebrates each person's individuality and uniqueness. Jacqueline not only challenges both pastors and people in their faith, but she encourages them to see themselves in a different light, with a renewed sense of wonder and joy for themselves and heir relationship with Jesus.

Jacqueline Loh, B.A B.L.Arch
Founder/President/ Author

Bishop Ronald Gilmore

... is from the Diocese of Dodge City Kansas. He was ordained in 1969 in the Diocese of Wichita, Kansas and served as priest, professor, chaplain, chancellor and Vicar General. He was then Bishop of Dodge City from 1998 – 2011. A gifted and prolific writer, and effective story teller, his greatest strength is his ability to lead us into a simpler form of prayer: to let the Spirit pray within a person, and to engage parishioners in a series of conversations about Wonder. Bishop Gilmore's presentation style is candid, poetic, and heart touching. He recently published three books from 2016 – 2018: they say how it was to be one Bishop, in one place, in one time.

Bishop Ronald M. Gilmore
Spiritual Director, Vice President

For more information on how to invite us to your parish to give a retreat, how to inquire about our workshops, or how to order our materials and how to become a sponsor for our ministry:

Please Write, and our web site:

✉ Address:

Grace that Reigns Society USA
2002 Fairway Drive
Dodge City, Kansas
67801 U.S.A

🌐 Web Site:

http://www.GracethatReigns.com

f Facebook:

https://www.facebook.com/GracethatReigns

@ Please Contact:

Jacqueline Loh
Email: **Jacqueline@GracethatReigns.com**

Bishop Ronald M. Gilmore
Email: **rmg@dcdiocese.org**

" For I know the Plans I have for You. Plans to give you hope and a future. "

Jeremiah 29:11